The Food Pyramid

by Janine Scott

Content and Reading Adviser: Mary Beth Fletcher, Ed.D.
Educational Consultant/Reading Specialist
The Carroll School, Lincoln, Massachusetts

Spyglass
BOOKS

COMPASS POINT BOOKS

Minneapolis, Minnesota

Compass Point Books
3109 West 50th Street, #115
Minneapolis, MN 55410

Visit Compass Point Books on the Internet at *www.compasspointbooks.com*
or e-mail your request to *custserv@compasspointbooks.com*

Photographs ©: Rubberball Productions, cover; PhotoDisc, cover; Comstock, cover, 4; U.S. Department
of Agriculture, 5, 8, 12, 16 (inset, right); Unicorn Stock Photos/Carol Prange, 6; Phil Bulgasch, 7;
Owen Franken/Corbis, 9; Unicorn Stock Photos/Ronald E. Partis, 10; Roy Morsch/Corbis, 11; Photo
Network/Esbin-Anderson, 13; Unicorn Stock Photos/Jim Shippee, 14; Brand X Pictures, 15; Photo
Network/Grace Davies, 16; D.S. Kerr/Visuals Unlimited, 16, (inset, left); Ariel Skelley/Corbis, 17;
Gary W. Carter/Visuals Unlimited, 18 (left); Patti McConville/The Image Finders, 18 (right);
LWA-Sharie Kennedy/Corbis, 19.

Project Manager: Rebecca Weber McEwen
Editors: Heidi Schoof and Patricia Stockland
Photo Researcher: Svetlana Zhurkina
Designer: Jaime Martens
Illustrator: Anna-Maria Crum

Library of Congress Cataloging-in-Publication Data
Scott, Janine.
 The food pyramid / by Janine Scott.
  p. cm. — (Spyglass books)
Includes index.
Contents: Food for fuel—The food pyramid—Fruits and vegetables—Bread, pasta, noodles—Cereals
and rice—Milk and milk products—Eggs, meat, and nuts—Oils, fats, and sweets—On our plates.
 ISBN 0-7565-0447-3
 1. Nutrition—Juvenile literature. 2. Food—Juvenile literature.
 [1. Nutrition. 2. Food.] I. Title. II. Series.
 QP141 .S349 2003
 613.2—dc21   2002012624

Contents

NOTE: Glossary words are in **bold** the first time they appear.

Food for Life

Food gives our bodies *energy.*

To stay healthy, we need to eat many different kinds of foods.

Too much of any one kind of food can be unhealthy.

5

The Food Pyramid

A food pyramid shows us what kinds of food we should eat each day.

Bread and Pasta, Cereals and Rice

The bottom of the pyramid shows what foods we should eat the most. We should eat bread and pasta.

Bread and pasta give our bodies energy.

We should also eat *cereals* and rice. They help our bodies stay healthy.

Cereals and rice have *fiber.* Fiber helps food move through our bodies.

Fruits and Vegetables

We should eat fruits and vegetables.
They give our bodies quick energy.

Fruits and vegetables have many *vitamins* and *minerals.*

Milk and Milk Products

The middle of the food pyramid shows foods that we should eat in smaller amounts. We should eat milk, cheese, and yogurt.

Milk, cheese, and yogurt keep our bones and teeth healthy.

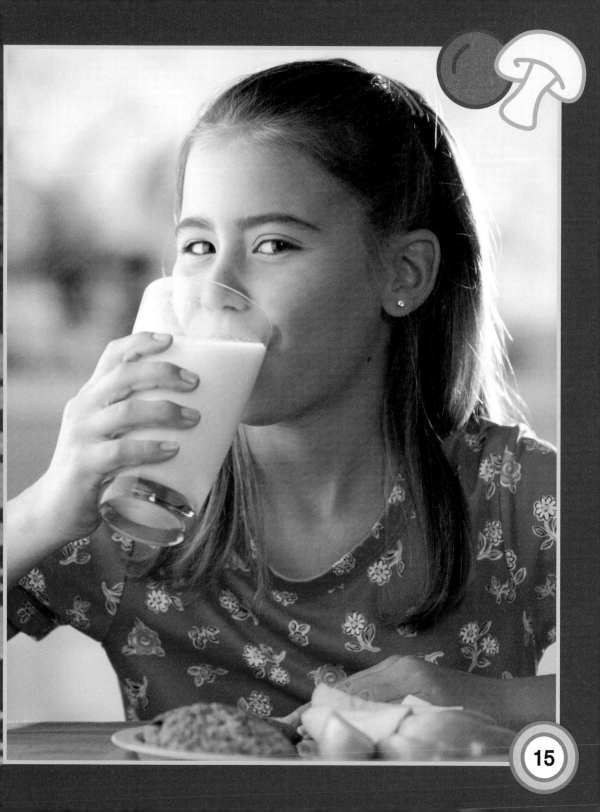

Eggs, Meat, and Nuts

We should eat eggs, meat, and nuts. They help our bodies grow big and strong.

Eggs, meat, and nuts help to build and *repair* the body.

Oils, Fats, and Sugars

The top of the food pyramid shows foods we should eat in very small amounts.

Desserts can be full of sugar and fat.

The body stores fat that it does not use.

On Our Plates

To stay healthy, we need to eat the right kinds of foods.
We also need to eat the right amounts.

Don't eat much of this

Eat some of this

Eat some of this

Eat a lot of this

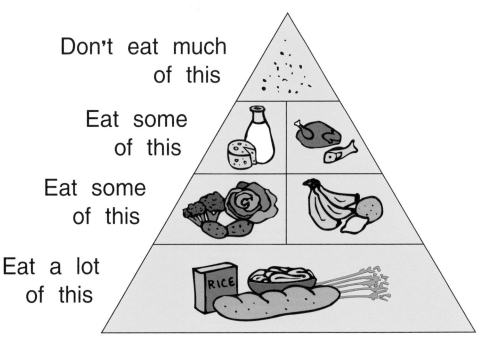

Breakfast

Lunch

Dinner

21

Glossary

cereal–a grain grown for food, such as wheat, corn, or rice

energy–a force that gives something the power to grow or move

fiber–a part of some foods that passes through the body but is not digested

mineral–something found in nature that is not an animal or a plant

repair–to make something work again, or to put back together something that is broken

vitamin–something in food that is needed for good health

Learn More

Books

Bagley, Katie. *Eat Right: Tips for Good Nutrition.* Mankato, Minn.: Bridgestone Books, 2002.

Frost, Helen. *Eating Right (The Food Guide Pyramid.)* Mankato, Minn.: Pebble Books, 2000.

McGinty, Alice B. *Staying Healthy: Eating Right.* New York: PowerKids Press, 1997.

Web Sites

ABC Kids

www.ext.nodak.edu/food/kidsnutrition/ kids-2.htm

Kids Food Cyberclub

www.kidfood.org/kf_cyber.html

Index

GR: I
Word Count: 155

From Janine Scott

I live in New Zealand and have two daughters. They love to read books that are full of fun facts and features. I hope you do, too!

24